AF207699

The Girl with the Magic Ponytails

Karen J Young

illustrations by Yoko Matsuoka

The Girl with the Magic Ponytails
copyright 2020 Karen J. Young

ISBN: 978-0-578-55090-9

First published in 2020 by Huqua Press
An operating unit of Morling Manor Corporation
Los Angeles, California

Graphic Design: designSimple

thegirlwiththemagicponytails.com

For Rachel,
whose ponytails
and special magic
inspired this book

Riley has super long
chocolate-brown hair
that she keeps in two
neatly gathered ponytails,
one on each side
of her head.

Even as a baby,
Riley sprouted
itty-bitty ponytails.

On her birthday,
Riley wears
razzle-dazzle
super-duper
extra-special
ponytails.

They're not low ponytails.

They're not high ponytails.

They're
in-the-middle,
just-right
ponytails.

LIBRARY

Wherever she goes, people say,
"Hey, you're Riley.
The ponytail girl."

Riley would not, could not,
ever be seen without
her ponytails!

That's because her ponytails hold
an extraordinary secret kind
of magic that can *only* be unlocked by
her colossal imagination.

With a flip and a twirl, a twist and
a pull, Riley's ponytails can turn
ordinary days into fantastical
adventures.

She can
blast off
like a rocket
to the
moon.

She can fly
like a bird
through
the clouds.

She can
jump over
the ribbons
of a rainbow.

She can swing
from
tree to tree
in the
jungle.

She can
sail a ship
on the
high seas.

She can
grab onto a
star way up high
in the sky.

She can conduct an orchestra...
and hit a home run.

She can

paint a

kaleidoscopic

sunset.

She can
put out a fire...
and make a
garden grow.

She can
warm herself
in the cold of
winter.

And she can
fan herself
in the heat
of summer.

She can
help her friends
when
spring showers.

And she can
rake a neighbor's yard
bursting with
fall colors.

She can twist and turn
through time
and space,
sometimes landing in a
long-ago place.

And best of all, she can hug
the entire planet
with one gigantic,
bigger-than-
anything-you've-
ever-seen
embrace!

Wherever she goes,
whatever she does,
Riley wears ponytails.

They're not
low ponytails.

They're not
high ponytails.

They're
in-the-middle, just-right

ponytails.

Printed in the USA
CPSIA information can be obtained
at www.ICGtesting.com
LVHW060822181223
766490LV00014B/521